A First Look at
Fairies

by Emma Carlson-Berne

LERNER PUBLICATIONS ◆ MINNEAPOLIS

To Elise

Note to Educators

Throughout this book, you'll find critical-thinking questions. These can be used to engage young readers in thinking critically about the topic and in using the text and photos to do so.

Lerner Publications Company
An imprint of Lerner Publishing Group, Inc.
241 First Avenue North
Minneapolis, MN 55401 USA

For reading levels and more information, look up this title at www.lernerbooks.com.

Main body text set in Helvetica Textbook Com Roman.
Typeface provided by Linotype AG.

Designer: Lauren Cooper
Lerner team: Martha Kranes

Library of Congress Cataloging-in-Publication Data

Names: Carlson-Berne, Emma, 1979– author.
Title: A first look at fairies / Emma Carlson-Berne.
Description: Minneapolis : Lerner Publications, [2021] | Series: Bumba books. Fantastic creature | Includes bibliographical references and index. | Audience: Ages 4–7 | Audience: Grades K–1 | Summary: "With carefully leveled text and a close text-to-photo match, emergent readers will delight in learning the different stories people have told about fairies throughout history."— Provided by publisher.
Identifiers: LCCN 2019044211 (print) | LCCN 2019044212 (ebook) | ISBN 9781541596825 (lib. bdg.) | ISBN 9781541599734 (eb pdf)
Subjects: LCSH: Faries—Juvenile literature.
Classification: LCC GR549 .B47 2020 (print) | LCC GR549 (ebook) | DDC 398/.45—dc23

LC record available at https://lccn.loc.gov/2019044211
LC ebook record available at https://lccn.loc.gov/2019044212

Manufactured in the United States of America
1-47788-48228-11/15/2019

Table of Contents

Fairies!

Imagine a fairy. Do you think of a tiny, magical person with wings?

Fairies are not real. But

people imagine they are.

Fairies look like tiny humans who can fly. They might have arms, legs, and wings. They also might have magic wands.

What would a fairy wear?

In some stories, fairies are

tiny and live underground.

They might live in a mine

and help the miners.

Some say that fairies live in people's homes. They might do housework. They might watch over the home.

Long ago, people told stories about dangerous fairies. They said fairies could turn milk rotten or trap travelers in bogs.

Sometimes, people called

fairies little people or hidden

people. Some people

thought they were angels.

Other times, people said that fairies were the spirits of things from nature. They might live in flowers.

Where else might a fairy live?

We can have fun imagining
stories about lots of fairies!

Fairy Diagram

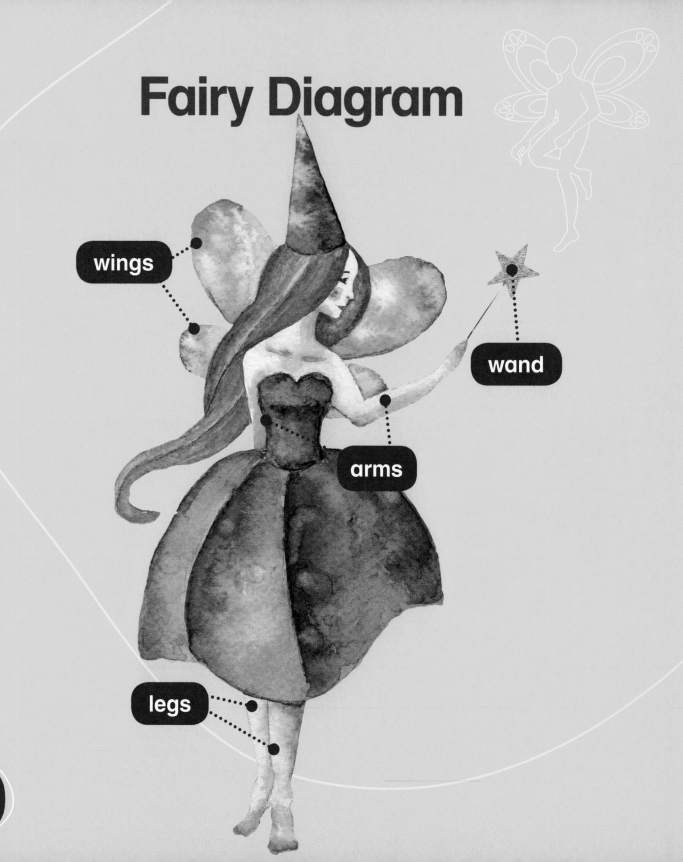

wings

wand

arms

legs

Picture Glossary

bogs

wet parts of the ground that are too soft to walk on

housework

tasks in a home, such as doing dishes or laundry

magical

something that is not real and has special powers

mine

an underground tunnel where people dig up rocks

23

Read More

Carlson-Berne, Emma. *A First Look at Unicorns*. Minneapolis: Lerner Publications, 2021.

Dinmont, Kerry. *Homes Past and Present*. Minneapolis: Lerner Publications, 2019.

Murray, Laura K. *Fairies: Are They Real?* Mankato, MN: Creative Education, 2017.

Index

Photo Credits